GETTING TO KNOW
THE U.S. PRESIDENTS

# JAMES A.
# GARFIELD

TWENTIETH PRESIDENT
1881

WRITTEN AND ILLUSTRATED BY MIKE VENEZIA

CHILDREN'S PRESS®
A DIVISION OF SCHOLASTIC INC.
NEW YORK   TORONTO   LONDON   AUCKLAND   SYDNEY
MEXICO CITY   NEW DELHI   HONG KONG
DANBURY, CONNECTICUT

Reading Consultant: Nanci R. Vargus, Ed.D., Assistant Professor, School of Education, University of Indianapolis

Historical Consultant: Marc J. Selverstone, Ph.D., Assistant Professor, Miller Center of Public Affairs, University of Virginia

Photographs © 2006: Bridgeman Art Library International Ltd., London/New York/Richard Morris Hunt/Vanderbilt Cottage, Newport, Rhode Island/Boltin Picture Library: 4; Corbis Images: 5, 7 left, 19, 27, 31, 32 (Bettmann), 6 (Schenectady Museum/Hall of Electrical History Foundation), 3; Getty Images/Hulton Archive: 8 (James Hope/MPI), 26 (MPI), 28, 29 (Stock Montage), 7 right; Library of Congress: 24 (Kurz & Allison), 17; North Wind Picture Archives: 10, 14, 21; Ohio Historical Society/James A. Garfield Presidential Collection: 12; Stock Montage, Inc.: 20.

Colorist for illustrations: Dave Ludwig

Library of Congress Cataloging-in-Publication Data

Venezia, Mike.
    James A. Garfield / written and illustrated by Mike Venezia.
        p. cm. — (Getting to know the U.S. presidents)
    ISBN 0-516-22625-8 (lib. bdg.)   0-516-25403-0 (pbk.)
    1. Garfield, James A. (James Abram), 1831-1881—Juvenile literature. 2.
Presidents—United States—Biography—Juvenile literature. I. Title.
    E687.V46 2006
    973.8'4'092–dc22
                                    2005012083

1 2 3 4 5 6 7 8 9 10 R 15 14 13 12 11 10 09 08 07 06

A photograph of President James A. Garfield

James Abrams Garfield, the twentieth president of the United States, was born in 1831 on a frontier farm in Cuyahoga County, Ohio. James was the last president to have been born in a log cabin. He has always been admired for climbing his way out of poverty to become a successful teacher, educator, preacher, Civil War hero, and national leader.

James A. Garfield became president in 1881. It was a time in American history that was so remarkable it has two names. This period is known as both the Gilded Age and the Age of Extremes.

Gilded objects are objects coated with a thin layer of gold. It's not that everything was covered in gold during this time, but that

In the late 1800s, families like the Vanderbilts showed off their wealth by living in elegant homes (above) and dressing their children in fancy, expensive clothing (top photo on opposite page).

extremely rich people wanted to show off and make everything they owned look as expensive as possible. At the same time, there were many people in the United States who were so poor they could hardly afford food or clothes.

A poor family living in a one-room apartment in New York City in the 1890s

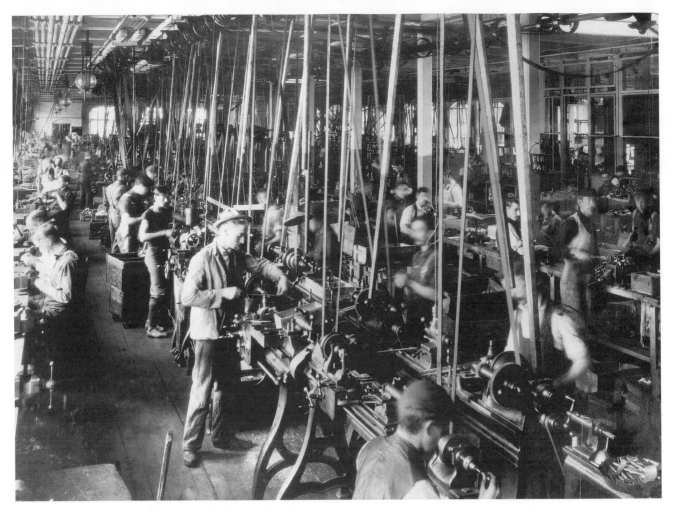

An American factory in the late 1800s

In the 1870s and 1880s, factories and big companies called corporations were growing extremely fast. Hundreds of thousands of immigrants from all over the world came to the United States. They hoped to find jobs in factories, oil fields, and coal mines. Workers were needed to build railroads and bridges, too.

Many government officials at that time were greedy and crooked. Some tried to steal the public's money for themselves. New inventions such as the typewriter, telephone, light bulb, and phonograph were coming out all the time. It was an exciting time, filled with extreme changes, both good and bad.

Alexander Graham Bell's telephone (left) and Thomas Edison's light bulb (right) were two of the many important inventions of the late 1800s.

An illustration showing the log cabin in which James A. Garfield was born

James was the youngest in the family. His mother was amazed at how big he was when he was born. He weighed 10 pounds! James' family may have been the poorest of any president's.

When James was only two years old, his father died. Mrs. Garfield and her older children worked their farmland and did their chores as well as they could.

James was too young to work. He did go to school, though. His sister Hatti began carrying him to school when he was three. James was very intelligent. He began reading the Bible soon after he started his classes.

This hand-colored woodcut from the 1800s shows a young James A. Garfield working as a mule rider towing a canal boat in Ohio.

James didn't like farm work at all while he was growing up. He spent as much time as possible reading. His favorite stories were about sea adventures. James dreamed of becoming a sailor. When he was sixteen, he left home, against his mother's wishes, to find a job on the waterfront in Cleveland, Ohio.

When James was rudely turned away by an angry, drunken sea captain, he gave up the idea of working on a ship for the time being. Instead, he got a job driving mules that pulled canal boats. Because he was always day dreaming about life on the sea, James ended up falling into the canal fourteen times! Finally, he came down with a bad fever and had to return home.

Mrs. Garfield spent months nursing her son back to health. During this time, she tried to convince James how important it was to get a good education. She told him that even sailors needed an education. James finally agreed to go to a nearby academy.

At first, he wasn't impressed at all with his new school. James already knew the simple lessons that were being taught during the first term. It seemed as if teachers there didn't know much more than the students. But then something happened that changed James Garfield's life forever. The classes eventually improved, and James found that he loved to learn.

In the early 1850s, James studied at the Western Reserve Eclectic Institute (now Hiram College) in Hiram, Ohio.

James learned Latin, science, and algebra quickly at the academy. By the time he was eighteen, he was teaching younger students at the school. Now James had a way of making money so he could continue his education. He also worked as a carpenter to make extra cash.

After he left the academy, James became a student at the Western Reserve Eclectic Institute in Hiram, Ohio. Mrs. Garfield couldn't afford to send her son any money at all. James was willing to do almost anything to continue his education, so he took a job as the school janitor.

The Eclectic Institute was a religious school. Religion was very important to James. While he worked and studied, he began to preach at local churches on Sunday.

James Garfield was an excellent preacher. His words inspired many people. This talent would come in handy throughout his life.

Even though James was super busy, he still found time for fun. He enjoyed hunting, fishing, and going to parties.

James especially loved dating. For a while, he dated three girls at the same time! He finally asked Lucretia Rudolph to be his wife.

A portrait of Lucretia Rudolph Garfield

James Garfield finished his schooling at Williams College in Massachusetts. After graduating from there with honors in 1856, he returned to teach at his old school in Hiram, Ohio. He ended up becoming president of the Eclectic Institute at the age of twenty-six.

Around this time, James became interested in politics. Being from the northern state of Ohio, James had strong feelings against slavery. James was considered an abolitionist. Abolitionists hated slavery and wanted to see it stopped in southern states.

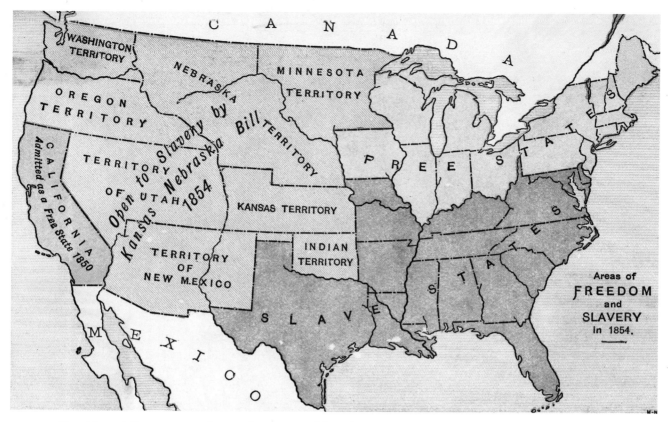

This United States map shows the areas of freedom and slavery in 1854.

They also wanted to prevent slavery from spreading to any new U.S. territories. James joined a new political group, called the Republican Party, which was against slavery. He then decided to run for Ohio state senator, and won his first election in 1859.

James A. Garfield campaigned for Abraham Lincoln (shown at left in this campaign poster) when Lincoln ran for president in 1860.

HON. ABRAHAM LINCOLN, OF ILLINOIS.

HON. HANNIBAL HAMLIN, OF MAINE,

FOR PRESIDENT.

FOR VICE PRESIDENT.

James loved his new job as senator. He decided that politics, not teaching or preaching, would be his career. In 1860, James Garfield used his talent as a speaker to help Abraham Lincoln get elected. He went from town to town giving inspiring speeches about Abe.

Soon after Lincoln was elected, southern states began to break away from the Union to form their own country. Southerners wanted to protect their right to own black slaves. This disagreement finally led to the bloody Civil War, which began on April 12, 1861.

The Civil War began when Confederate troops attacked Fort Sumter in 1861.

James Garfield was glad the war started. He felt it was the only way to end slavery. Right away, he volunteered to help fight. James was given an important assignment. His job was to recruit and train men to form the 42nd Ohio Infantry.

James went back to the college where he had taught and gave some rousing speeches. He urged students to fight for their country and gathered up hundreds of new recruits. James Garfield didn't really have any military experience. He used his teaching abilities and leadership skills to successfully train more than one thousand new soldiers.

Garfield fought bravely in a number of important Civil War battles, including the 1863 Battle of Chickamauga (above).

James was soon given the rank of colonel in the Union army. He and his men fought the Confederate army in the battles of Middle Creek, Shiloh, Corinth, and Chickamauga. Soon James was promoted to major general.

The Ohio State Legislature was so proud of James that they elected him to the U.S. House of Representatives.

At first, James didn't want to take the job. The war was still going on, and General Garfield didn't think he should leave the army. But President Lincoln convinced him that Congress needed a soldier who understood the army's needs. In 1863, James A. Garfield resigned from the military. He served in Congress for seventeen years and was re-elected eight times.

President Lincoln wanted to heal the nation and repair the terrible damage that had been done to the South (above). Congressman James A. Garfield was less forgiving. He thought the southern states should be punished for causing the war.

When the Civil War ended in 1865, President Lincoln hoped the North and South could be reunited in a peaceful way. Abraham Lincoln never got the chance to see if his plan, called Reconstruction, would work. On April 14, 1865, John Wilkes Booth shot President Lincoln. The president died the next morning.

James Garfield hadn't agreed with Abe Lincoln's plan. Congressman Garfield thought the southern states should be punished for causing the war. He wanted to force them to give former slaves equal rights, and he wanted the federal government to have strict control over southern state governments.

This illustration, from the late 1800s, shows Garfield as a strong supporter of the rights of newly freed slaves.

Abraham Lincoln

Andrew Johnson

During his seventeen years in Congress, James Garfield worked under four different presidents. They were Abraham Lincoln, Andrew Johnson, Ulysses S. Grant, and Rutherford B. Hayes. James probably learned more about how the U.S. government worked than any other president before him. It isn't surprising that many people were interested in having James Garfield as president someday.

In 1880, when he was nominated to run for president at the Republican National Convention, James Garfield was totally surprised. James never had any plans to become president of the United States. He agreed to run, though, and won the election.

Ulysses S. Grant

Rutherford B. Hayes

Right away, President Garfield was swamped by people who wanted government jobs. In those days, campaign workers who helped politicians get elected expected to be rewarded with jobs. It didn't matter if these people were qualified for the jobs they wanted. This method of rewarding people is called patronage. James Garfield hated the patronage system.

Even though lots of people were pressuring him, President Garfield often ignored job seekers who had no skills. Instead, he chose people who were well-trained and trustworthy.

Unfortunately, one man the president turned down for a job was a man named Charles Guiteau. One day, while the president waited for a train, the angry and insane Guiteau stepped out of the shadows and shot President Garfield in the back.

An illustration showing Charles Guiteau shooting President Garfield

Doctors couldn't find the bullet in the president's body. They made things worse by probing around his wound with unclean fingers. James Garfield got a serious infection. He died from blood poisoning about ten weeks later, on September 19, 1881. Charles Guiteau had been captured right away. He was found guilty and sentenced to hang.

No one knows what kind of president Garfield would have been. He had been president for only six months when he died.

James A. Garfield wanted to make the nation's economy strong, reduce corruption, and protect the rights of former slaves. He is respected for refusing to be pressured by others when making decisions for his country.